WHAT IF SHE KNEW SHE WAS POWERFUL

A REAL LIFE SUPERWOMAN

SHELIA LENORA JOHNSON PETERS

WHAT IF SHE KNEW SHE WAS POWERFUL

Stratton Press Publishing
831 N Tatnall Street Suite M #188,
Wilmington, DE 19801
www.stratton-press.com
1-888-323-7009

ISBN (Paperback): 978-1-64345-921-9
ISBN (Ebook): 978-1-64345-922-6

Printed in the United States of America

To my grandchildren:

Christopher, Ayesha, Tremelis, Rae'Chelle,
Area, Anya, Donatae, Paris, Annette, Angelique,
Joshua, Justus, Amarisa, Alijah, Alex, Daniel,
Jordan, Ayden, and great-granddaughter Milan

DEDICATION

First, I give honor and respect to my Lord and Savior, Jesus Christ, because it was through the cross that I learned the power of prayer. Without prayer, none of this would have been possible.

Secondly, I dedicate this book to my deceased mother, Mary Demeritte Neilly, who said a prophesy to me in 1995: "Shelia, you may be at the bottom with little now, but God is going to raise you up and give you so much more than others. People are going to be surprised of how God raised you up."

Thank you, Mary. God has raised me up. I am up.

Third, I dedicate this book to my most precious jewels—my children: Deborah, Bernadette, Margarita, Theresa, Edwin, Shay, Nicholas, and Erwin—who have blessed me with eighteen grandchildren. I love all of you. I would have died for you all if I had to.

Fourth, I dedicate this book to my sisters: Sandra, Winnie, and Fran and my brothers: Van, Alex, and Mannie. Thank you for being there for me and my eight children. God bless you all.

Last, but not least, I dedicate this book to my niece Antionette, who encouraged me in 1995 to write my life story. Thank you, Antionette. To my niece Vanteria, who typed my first manuscript, thank you.

FOREWORD

Shelia shares her life's struggles and triumphs in a candid way that will serve as a valuable resource for other battered women. Some people have been looking for love in all the wrong places. Some people have fallen for all the wrong people. One sees from the abused eyes the struggles that keep so many women in abusive relationships. Life's difficulties are unavoidable, and sooner or later, they touch each one of us. If you are one of those who is at the mercy of circumstances, I hope you are ready for a change and that you will read this book with an open mind. Remember, if what you have been doing in the past hasn't resulted in what you desired, then it is time to try a different approach. You don't have to just wait around hoping something great will happen! Avoid relationships with emotionally unhealthy persons.

—Elder Van G Neilly
Real estate consultant

Turning Your Stumbling Blocks
into Stepping-Stones!

With the hope of sharing this experience to enlighten and encourage other women, this story is written to tell the struggles of a woman living in an abusive marriage and the faith she had in God to step out of this situation. Hopefully, reading the book will inspire some person to change the course of her life and break free of this vicious (brutal) abusive cycle.

May the Holy Spirit guide you as you read this book and with a prayer that some weary abused soul will find the courage to be bold, to step out from a life of fear and take control, to help someone else turn their stumbling blocks into stepping-stones.

—Pastor Selwyn M. Scott

This book provides us with several types of books in one—drama, mystery, action, and comedy—because you will finally have a reason to laugh. It truly proves that the love between God and His faithful people far exceeds any man's abuse.

—Manfreth Neilly
Aspiring writer and editor of *Poetry, Slogans, Jingles and Short Stories*

INTRODUCTION

Living in the Bahamas was very rough for me. Don't get me wrong. There were a few good times but a lot more bad times. There were times when I was so depressed, I wanted to die. However, many times I cried out in desperation, and it seemed as if there was no way out. Here is my life story, the struggles I faced, and how the Lord brought me out.

CHAPTER 1

MY LIFE STORY IS MY LEGACY AND ACT OF LOVE

And it shall come to pass, when many evils
and troubles are befallen them, that this song
shall testify against them as a witness; for
it shall not be forgotten out of the mouths
of their seed: for I know their imagination
which they go about, even now, before I have
brought them into the land which I sware.

—Deuteronomy 31:21

I was fifteen years old when I started my first relationship. I was so in love that I wanted it to last for a lifetime. Erwin Bernard Johnson was the love of my life!

He was five feet, seven inches tall and had smooth skin, caramel in complexion, a six-pack to die for, and two hundred pounds of muscles. Whew! Looking at his physique would make any woman drool and any man jealous. His hands, however, were rough, but that only indicated that he was a hard-working man, something every woman wanted. Who was he, and how did I meet him?

Erwin was Big Jack's nephew. Big Jack was my mother's boyfriend at the time. When Big Jack met me, he thought I would be perfect for his nephew. Therefore, he took my picture with him when he went home to Long Island. He told Erwin that he found a nice, beautiful, decent girl for him to marry. Of course, every man wants to see what they are getting into. So Big Jack showed Erwin the picture. Once he saw my picture, he was impressed and wanted to meet me right away. Unfortunately, he was unable to travel at that time.

Shortly afterward, Erwin was in a fight in Long Island. Since there was no hospital on Long Island, Erwin had to be rushed to Nassau on the emergency flight. He was admitted in Princess Margaret Hospital with gunshot wounds from a BB gun. The wounds were not serious but still required medical attention. When Big Jack found out that his nephew was in the hospital, he took me with him to meet Erwin. Although Erwin was lying there in pain, I could not help but admire the fine-looking young man looking back at me. I knew within myself that he felt the same attraction for me that I felt for him, but we did not exchange much conversation at that time. The very next day, however, I could not wait to see him. So I went to the hospital by myself to visit Erwin, of course, with my mother's permission. During those times, a young lady was not allowed to go out or to go see a young man without her mother's permission. That was the rule that we all lived by.

When I got there, Erwin was discharged from the hospital. We both walked from the hospital to my mother's house. He was so smooth and slick. He took my hand and held it in his. Then he said, "My hand too rough to hold your hand. It would hurt your hand."

I looked at him and smiled like any teenager would. He walked me back to my mother's house, and then he left. The very next week, we started dating.

CHAPTER 2

THE BLIND YOUNG WOMAN

Beware lest any man spoil you through philosophy and vain deceit, after the tradition of men, after the rudiments of the world, and not after Christ.

—Colossians 2:8

The islands did not have as much entertainment as America has today.

Therefore, we had to make the best out of the little entertainment we had. Fortunately, we were both equally interested in each other, so just being in each other's company was good enough for us. We went to the movies, and sometimes we went dancing. All eyes were on us. I was so petite, and he was so huge that it looked as if he was "robbing the cradle," as some might say. We were like Beauty and the Beast. The only difference was he was a good-looking beast. As was standard practice, my mother always went with us when we went dancing. It was not that she did not trust me; it was just that no mother trusts any man with her young daughter.

Fifteen in my days was the age that every girl starts thinking about dating. If she was not thinking it, her parents were planning for it. Marriage was nowhere near my mind. I was just happy to be a year older and excited to receive my first gift from my boyfriend. Well, you know men; once they claim you to be their woman, they buy you anything you want, especially if they want something in return.

The story has not changed; even today some men are still the same.

Once they purchase a gift for you, you are officially theirs. Since it was my birthday, Erwin bought me a bush jacket. That was the style back then. I felt bad just taking a gift from him when I did not have anything to give him in return. When I offered to buy him a gift, he said, "You do not have to buy me anything. Just give me some sex."

This man was either stupid or just plain bold. Shocked by his response, I did not know what to do. I was scared for two reasons: one reason being I heard that sex hurts very badly and the second reason being that a girl can get pregnant.

Confused and scared, I went to my cousin Mel for advice. It was a horrible idea, but hey, she was a little older, so I thought she would have sound advice. I told her how I felt, and she told me I was stupid. "It is not going to hurt!" she assured me.

Of course, she already had a baby boy. So I thought she, of all people, should know whether it hurt or not hurt. A few thoughts crossed my mind. I thought, *She looks happy. She is not sick or dead, so it must be okay.*

That night, scared as a rat about to be fed to a snake, I went out with Erwin. He took me to a hotel. To this day, I do not know where it was. I was so afraid of what was about to happen and what would happen to me if my mother found out. Fear took a hold of me so badly that I could not remember the looks or the smell of the hotel. It could have been some snake hole in the back of a bush for all I knew. Well, we walked into the room. I remember he had a smile on his face. I tried to find comfort in his smile but could not find any.

Then in a moment, he took my virginity. He was not gentle at all. He was very rough! As I could remember, it hurt so badly. I knew he must have injured me in some way. That night, I saw the beast eyes stare right into my eyes. At that moment, my body became paralyzed. I wanted to scream, "Please stop! You are hurting me," but my body could not send the message to my brain fast enough. So I got lost mentally. I drifted off to a place that kept my mind occupied until it was over. I wanted to cry, but I had to act like a woman and suck it up. The tears in my tear glands were frozen with fear that if they showed up, he might hurt me even more.

Some might say, what about foreplay? Yeah, right! During that time, foreplay was not in his vocabulary and definitely not mine. I barely knew about sex, much less foreplay. I remember when I was walking back home, I could hardly walk. I felt like I had a ghastly case of the chafes. At that moment, I did not realize how that night affected me mentally and physically. I did not know any better, so I figured this is what being a woman is about.

When I got back to the house, I saw the red eyes, black suit, sticky horns, and the long fork with sharp points dancing in victory. Mel was grinning; she was so happy I was like her now. I was no longer a virgin. It is amazing how people can give you awful advice so that you can be like them. I thought she had my best interests at heart, but I soon found out that she just wanted the negative attention transferred off her and onto someone else, and I was the guinea pig.

As time went on, we continued to have sex, as Erwin wanted it. I was never enjoying it; it always hurt because mentally, I never got over the first time. There was never any fun in it for me, which led me to believe that sex was only for men. The pleasure of having my body caressed by his hands, his lips gently touching mine, the ecstasy of having my nipples stimulated by the one I loved was never a gratification of mine. Sex in my vocabulary was just a "slam, bam, I am the man" event. Yeah! Good job, woman, now grab me my beer and a cigarette.

I wish I had listened to my mother. Just like every young girl, I thought my mom wanted to get into my business to stop me from having fun. I remember my mom saying to me, "If Erwin ever put any question to you, you must let me know."

Now Erwin asked me many questions. I remember one evening we went to the movie, and when we got back home, Erwin asked me a question. I kissed my teeth. The act of kissing my teeth means to express disapproval, contempt, or dissatisfaction with a situation or person by making a sound through the act of sucking air through one's teeth. What did I do that for? He slapped me, one hard backhand slap; I felt my head spinning around, my face turning red, and my ear ringing.

I knew for sure that was the question my mom was talking about, so I turned to run inside to tell my mother, Mary. He grabbed me by the hand, held me back, and kissed me. I don't remember if he apologized to me, but like every foolish woman, I never told anyone, especially my mother. So I was back to, which one of the questions should I let her know about? Definitely, I was not going to talk about sex with my mother. Which teenage girl in her right mind would talk to her mother about sex? Yeah, we will talk about marriage and school but never sex. It was a sin!

There are many things I should have told Mary, but I did not. Had I confided in her, she would have revealed to me the beast that Erwin was. My silence about the first sign of abuse led me into the life that was to follow. So many times as women, we allow fear to get us into predicaments of bondage. We find ourselves in jail, serving a life sentence with no parole, and our boyfriend, lover, sweetheart, or husband is the nasty warden. If we can only remember that God said in His word that He did not give us the spirit of fear but of power, love, and a sound mind. We can walk away from any fearful situation. God did not promise us a life of bondage. He said in His Word that he who the Son has set free is free indeed. Yes, we are free!

About three months later, Mary, noticed a change in my body. She took me to the doctor and found out I was pregnant. At that moment, I wished I had told her instead of Mel about the question. It was then that I realized what question she was talking about. Why didn't she just say, "Shelia, if Erwin asks you to have sex with him, say no and come tell me"? I probably would not have been in the situation I was in had I spoken to her.

Unfortunately, the damage had already been done, and now I had to live with the consequences. Mothers, please be direct with your daughters because the little boys, soon-to-be men, will be direct with them and then smoothly ease their way into your daughter's heart and then their bed.

CHAPTER 3

A FAMILY TRIBUTE

Be ye not unequally yoked together with unbelievers: for what fellowship hath righteousness with unrighteousness? And what communion hath light with darkness?

—2 Corinthians 6:14

When the doctor told Mary I was pregnant, she told Erwin that he had to marry me. It was customary that if a man got any decent girl pregnant out of wedlock, he was obligated to marry her. Did I have a choice? I made my choice the night I got pregnant. Mothers back then were more concerned about covering up the shame of having a pregnant unmarried daughter than the happiness of the daughter. Therefore, Erwin and I got engaged in 1964. Erwin had Big Jack, his uncle, to write a letter asking or requesting to marry me. That made no sense to me because I had to marry him anyway, so a letter would make no difference. Big Jack was also my mother's boyfriend at that time.

What was I thinking? This man could not even write a letter requesting my hand in marriage. So what made me think he would be able to take care of me and a family? In addition, he slapped me once before. Did I really believe that slap was a one-time thing? Besides, we have not had one enjoyable sexual encounter. Would marriage make it any better? Yet in March of 1964 we announced that we were engaged and that we were getting married. Erwin gave me the money to pay for my wedding dress. Being the petite young lady I was, the dress was too big. His sister Loretta, who was a seamstress, took it and altered it to my fit. Big Jack gave Mary the money to pay for the wedding reception, including the food and drink.

I was the first in my family to have a wedding, so it was a big thing. I was going to become Mrs. Johnson, but little did I know what was ahead of me. I did not know what love was, and everything happened so fast. One minute I was dating, two minutes later I was having sex, and within a second, I was pregnant. Before I could count the minutes, I was married, and within an hour, I was a mother. The wedding day finally came. We got married on June 1, 1964. Three days after I got married, I was in the hospital having a miscarriage—*three days*. If I had only waited. Was God punishing me for all the wrong I had done?

After I came out of the hospital, I went to stay with Mary for a while, and Erwin came and stayed there. In the meantime, Big Jack and Mary had a fight; they terminated their relationship. Mary told me to leave Erwin because he was just like his uncle, saying, "They like to beat on women." They take pleasure in knowing that you feel helpless, hopeless, and dependent on them. Tell me why parents do things like that. They cover up useful information that could save their children a lot of heartache and pain just because they want to spare themselves some embarrassment.

Mary knew Erwin was just like his uncle, yet she still allowed us to get married simply because I was pregnant. Furthermore, she dated Big Jack for such a long time, and although he abused her, she never said a word. That is why so many women continue to be abused; they hide the abuse to save themselves the embarrassment of someone finding out. Had my mother told me about Big Jack before the wedding, I would have waited. Yeah right! We all know very well that when we are in love and our parents try to warn us about the man, we always say our parents do not want us to have any fun. So even if she had warned me, I still would have gotten married. Despite all the obvious signs of abuse, I was in love—at least I thought I was.

CHAPTER 4

A WIFE'S DENIAL

This day will I begin to put the dread of thee and the fear of thee upon the nations that are under the whole heaven, who shall hear report of thee, and shall tremble, and be in anguish because of thee.

—Deuteronomy 2:25

The nightmare began, and it was not the nice fairy tale we all read about. Instead, Beauty had turned into the ugly duckling, and Beast became a ferocious, hungry lion, prancing through the forest, ready to rip apart and devour his prey. Did I stand a chance at life? I do not know what happened to the kindhearted man I dated, but it seems as if as soon as he took my virginity, he took my senses.

One evening, Erwin and I were talking about his mother, who at the time was in the hospital. He asked me if I went to see her. I told him no. He slapped me, and I fell on the ground. I never knew a person should be punished for telling the truth. Had I known, I would have kindly smiled and said, "Yes, honey, she is doing much better than before."

Anyway, on the floor, I heard him say, "Get up." His voice was as cold as an iceberg. If the *Titanic* was still around, he could have sunk it in half the time the real iceberg sunk it. My whole body shook with fear. It was as if his voice set off an earthquake. I wish it had so that the earth could have swallowed me whole. At least I would have avoided what was about to happen. Of course, there was a battle going on in my mind. If I got up, he would only lick me back down to the ground. Yet if I did not get up at his command, only God knows what he was going to do. Before I got a chance to respond, he grabbed me up and put me on the bed. Just as he raised his fist to knock the daylight out of me, Mary, my mother, heard me crying and came to my rescue. He denied hurting me. How cold could a human being be?

How dare he looked my mother in her eyes and lie so blatantly? Did I mean anything to him? Was I of any value to him? Maybe I was just his punching bag that he used during practice to prepare him for the fight of life! My mother begged me to leave Erwin. I was afraid to leave him. I was in love with Erwin—at least I thought I was. I did not want to leave him.

Jesus suffered many things for us because He loves us. So why can't I just suffer these few things for the one I love? So I did not listen to my mother. Like a stubborn child, I stayed. I failed to realize that

Jesus suffered for us so that we do not have to suffer. He was whipped until the skin on His back tore. He was whipped so that I do not have to be whipped by any man. He suffered the pain and agony of thorns being pierced through His head so that I do not have to suffer any piercing. He did it for me, and yes, He did it for you.

When Erwin heard Mary telling me to leave him, he moved out. He thought she would do something to hurt him. Apparently, Big Jack got an apartment after he and Mary broke up, and Erwin moved in with him and left me at Mary's. Shortly afterward, Big Jack told him, "Go and get your wife." Women, your man will seek counsel from someone. Nine times out of ten, the counsel will not be in your best interest.

You must also seek counsel, but seek it from God. Listen to His voice; it will save your life! Erwin came back to the house and told me to come with him, so I left with him and moved in with him at Big Jack's apartment. Moving in with him and Big Jack was the biggest mistake of my life. I am now living with two abusers. Did I think it would get better? Obviously, I was not thinking! This was in 1964. Erwin, in the beginning, took me with him everywhere he went. Then he stopped, and I would be home in that apartment by myself until evening when Erwin came home from work.

In August of 1964, I got pregnant again. Big Jack moved out and left us there. I was not working, and Erwin was not making enough money to pay the rent, so we moved in with Auntie Ethlyn, her mother, her husband, and her daughter. They were living in a two-bedroom house. She put a single bed in the kitchen for me and Erwin, and we stayed there until Debbie was born. After Debbie's birth in 1965, we started to plan to move. Erwin became very aggressive and did not want me to go anywhere.

I did not know moving means increase aggression and aggravation. I remember before we moved that I wanted to visit my mother, and he was upset. Why would he get so angry about me going to visit my mother? Auntie Ethlyn had to speak to him and told him it was wrong for him to stop me from going to see my mother. I was very afraid of him because he would always threaten me and tell me what he would do to me if I left him. He boldly told me that I could not visit my mother anymore.

I went anyway. I remember going to Mary, my mother, and telling her what Erwin said. She was so mad she said he must be crazy to try to stop me from coming to see her. She then planned to send me away to the States to her sister Auntie Winnie. While she was making plans for my escape, I moved out of Auntie Ethlyn's house and back in with my mother and sisters and brothers. Then Erwin came by pleading to me to come back to him. Of course, he said he was sorry, and he wouldn't stop me from visiting my mom anymore. That is so typical of abusers!

Did I see the pattern? No, I was blinded by fear. I believed him and went back to him. In the meantime, he leased a piece of land on Farrington

Road near his sister's home and built a two-bedroom house with an outside toilet. Let's face it, we were poor. In November 1966, I got pregnant again with the third baby, which was Bernie. I went in the hospital and had Bernie at seven months; she was less than five pounds, so they kept her in the hospital for three weeks until she was five pounds. She came home by the time we were living in the house on Farrington Road. Shortly after that, I got pregnant again and had my fourth baby, Margarita, in 1967. She was also less than five pounds, so they kept her in the hospital about three weeks until she was weighed five pounds. Then she came home. At the same time, my sister-in-law, Loretta, was having a baby every year, and also my neighbor was having a baby every year, so I fit right in.

One worry after another appeared in my life. There is a saying in the Bahamas, "Must Jesus bear the cross alone and all the world go free? There is a cross for you, and there is a cross for me." I am convinced that I was bearing everyone's cross. My husband started drinking more and staying out late at night. He became more aggressive, and I became more afraid and depressed. I walked with my head hung low. I no longer saw the beauty in me. My face was trying to decide which complexion I was born with: black, blue, red, or even-tone brown. It was no use asking me because all I knew was black and blue. I began to work, but shortly afterward, I got pregnant again for the fourth time. Stupid, stupid, idiotic, crazy, glutton for punishment! Could you please tie them tubes up and save your kids from watching this abuse? The following year, 1968, I had another baby, Theresa, who was born in August. I was tired and did not want any more children. My body needed some rest. I went on the birth control pill because the church I was attending did not believe in having your tubes tied or in taking birth control pills, but I did the pill anyway. At least I had some time for my body to relax from having children, but not from the abuse.

CHAPTER 5

STRANGE STRATEGIES FOR SUCCESS

And if he shall neglect to hear them, tell it unto the church: but if he neglect to hear the church, let him be unto thee as an heathen man and a publican.

—Matthew 18:17

Church was a form of escape for my children and me. We were not afforded the opportunity to explore anywhere else. At least for a moment, I could escape to a place where I was told of a better place. How I longed to go to heaven. In the meantime, I enjoyed sitting back and listening to my pastor as he told me that the trials of this life are only there to make me strong. My pastor's words encouraged me to hold on because God was going to answer my prayers. He said to never give up because heaven would surely be worth it all. I knew for certain God was not going to answer one of my prayers because

Erwin would be six feet deep if God did answer my prayers. Yet I held on and trusted God for some form of release. I remember when Debbie was about four years old, I sent her to YPE (Young People Endeavor) with Loretta's children. Erwin came home, and he was mad. He made me drive to the church to get his child because she was too young to be at church. I was so afraid and angry, but I dared not show my anger. So like a little girl, I hid my feelings and obediently went to get his child. How could he do this? He just swiped away the one thing that brought happiness to our home.

Another time, Thelma and her husband came and picked me and the children up to spend the day with them. We came back home at around 9:00 p.m., and Erwin was lying on the couch drunk. I was praying that this would be one of the nights he stayed out late. Unfortunately for me, when I opened the door, the big bad wolf was staring me right in the face. When I walked in, I was so terrified. He greeted Thelma and her husband, Quinton, then he said, "Shelia has to tell me where she been." Quinton laughed and said, "You need to go to sleep and talk in the morning."

I thought all was fine and dandy. Shortly after they left, I was making a bottle of milk. He came into the kitchen and slapped me; the bottle went flying across the room. For a minute, I thought it was me flying. The milk spilled all over the place. The children in the room started crying. I was crying and shaking with fear. I blamed me for not standing up to him the first time. Now he feels like he can just knock me around when he feels like it. I was the ball, and he was the bat. Every time he stepped up to the plate, he was bound to hit a home run. The next morning when I woke up and looked in the mirror. I noticed my nose was swollen. He said he did not remember where I was, and he was sorry about what happened. I went to the doctor and had my nose checked out; it was not broken. Thank God.

Another time, Mass was having a birthday party for her husband; they were our neighbors, so they invited us to the party. My husband said he was going, but he did not arrive home yet, so I decided to go over there, which was right across the street. He came home shortly and saw me over there. He smiled and went into the house. As soon as I came home, he started beating me, asking me why I went over there.

For every slap, there was a negative connotation. For every punch, there was a degrading name. For every kick, there was an insult to my emotional stability. I saw my life crumbling right before my eyes. Who I was no longer existed. The neighbors heard and did nothing. Everyone was horrified of him. He was like the mean green giant that no one dare stand up to. He would squash anyone like a roach if they got in his way. Again, the next morning, he woke up and said he was sorry, he was not going to do it again. If I received a penny for every time I heard, "I am sorry, I will never do it again," I would be a millionaire. Ladies, an abusive man will always apologize, and a few minutes later, he will be back at the abuse. *Sorry* is not good enough if he is not seeking help for his problem. Unless he receives a complete transformation from God, he will not change. During this time, Erwin became more abusive and continued hitting on me. The hits became harder and more dangerous. My life was now in more danger than before. By this time, my mom had moved and gone to Miami with all the other children. I was alone.

Like I said before, my comfort came from going to church. My children and I were going to church very often with Loretta; we also attended midday prayer. I was not working, Loretta was a seamstress, and my neighbor was not working. We had a lot of time on our hands. I also had no money. I depended on my husband for everything. I would encourage every woman to get an education and have a job for herself. Everyone needs a sense of accomplishment. If you have to depend solely on someone to take care of you, he or she will always have you in bondage. Thank God my family in the States did not forget about me. They always sent clothes for the children. I remember our first television. My sister Sandra and brother Van bought it for us.

CHAPTER 6

A CHEMICAL IMBALANCE

Have mercy upon me, O Lord; consider my trouble which I suffer of them that hate me, thou that liftest me up from the gates of death.

—Psalm 9:13

The babies kept coming. I earned the title of baby-making machine. After two years on the pill, I went to the doctor. He told me I had to come off the pill because I could get a blood clot. He said that I had so many varicose veins, it could pose a problem to my health. Did he know what he was saying? I sure do hope so! I came off the pill and shortly afterward got pregnant again. This time, baby number six was a boy. Erwin was so glad, so I named him Edwin Bernard. I did not want to give him his dad's name. I was scared he would turn out like him.

Unfortunately for my baby but fortunately for me, Edwin had my personality. My husband was very angry with him, so he tried to make Edwin to be a hard, rough fighter. Regrettably, it did not happen, so he started to call Edwin a sissy. That hurt me so much, but I could not say anything. He would treat Edwin so bad. He called him all sorts of negative names and beat him for any little thing. I knew it was wrong, but I was too frightened to say anything. Besides, when I could not even defend myself, how could I defend my baby?

An alcoholic is a dangerous person. The slightest thing could trigger an alcoholic and cause some drastic results. Erwin was in the car driving; of course, he was drunk as a skunk. His friends were in the car with him. He tried to show that he had control over me, so he tried to talk to me while I was walking down the street toward the house. I would not talk to him because he was drunk and not making any sense. Why did I do that? When he came home that night, he beat me so badly. I had to run out of the house to save my life. That night, I am almost certain I slept literally in the dog house. I cried and cried and cried. God, all this time I had been in the church. Everyone knew what is happening, but nobody was doing anything to help me. My heart was aching and breaking. I knew I got myself into this situation, but whatever happened to Superman? Could I have a superhero to dig me and my children out of this hellhole? Jesus, when are You coming to my rescue?

Shortly afterward, I got pregnant again with my seventh baby, Shay. We decided it was enough, so I went on the pill again. We now have six babies living with us in a two-bedroom house. My God, please help us. Shortly after I had Shay, our children started visiting my mom and my siblings in the States every summer. The summer I went, I was pregnant again with my eighth baby. Two days after our trip, I came home and ended up in the hospital bleeding. I had a miscarriage at five months. That pregnancy almost killed me. I decided to have my tubes tied.

The night before the operation, I changed my mind and came out of the hospital.

As time went on, we realized that our two-bedroom house was too small for us. Therefore, we went to the bank and got a loan to buy a house, which we did get approved for. Unfortunately, our house burned down before we had a chance to move into our new home, so we were homeless for a while. Finally, we purchased a house on Carmichael Road; it had two bedrooms, one bathroom, a living room, a dining room, a den, and a kitchen. Yes, it was still two bedrooms, but we had more space. The house was under construction. My husband was supposed to finish the house, but he never did. We moved in anyway. When Edwin was about one year old, I started driving the school bus for our church school.

Shortly afterward, I got pregnant with my ninth baby, Nicholas. I continued driving the bus for the school. As tired as I was, Erwin would come home late at night drunk. Around two or three o'clock in the morning, he would tell me to get up out of the bed and prepare his dinner. When he was done eating his dinner, he would come into the room and throw the glass of water on me and start hitting on me and calling me names. I remember one night Erwin came home and woke me up and told me to get up and make up his dinner. I did.

Afterward, I went back to bed. He ate his dinner and then came in with a cold glass of water and threw it on me. He shouted, "Get up out of the bed, my wife, and talk to me."

What in the world could he possibly want to talk about at three o'clock in the morning? Reluctantly, I got up. At this point, I was prepared for anything. I had become used to the abuse. I just had to decide which side I wanted him to paint this time. He slapped me so hard that I screamed.

I did not know when the sound left my body. All I remember was Debbie, our oldest daughter, came running into the room screaming. He then slapped her and told her to never interfere when she sees him and her mother having something. That hurt me so bad, worse than the slap he gave me. As always, I was too afraid to do anything. As time went on, he continued to verbally and physically abuse Edwin, our oldest son. He thought this would make Edwin hard, but it was torture for me.

In addition, he would spend all his money before he came home, and sometimes there would be no money for food. Many times his mother had to give us groceries, or Auntie Ethelyn would bring food for us. This abuse continued during my pregnancy and went into my next pregnancy. I got pregnant again with my tenth baby shortly after Nicholas was born. By this time, my mind was made up; I was getting my tubes tied. So after I had my tenth baby, I got my tubes tied. We named our son Erwin Alexander. I came home to another scene in my life.

CHAPTER 7

THE ART OF STRATEGIC PRAYER AND SPIRITUAL WARFARE

But he is in one mind, and who can turn him?
And what his soul desireth, even that he doeth.

—Job 23:13

After the birth of my tenth baby, my tubes were tied. I was making frequent trips to the States. I began feeling a little better because I could not get pregnant anymore. Then I finally got a job working at the drive-in theater. I no longer had to go to my husband begging for money. Oh, the thrill he got out of watching me beg and plead. Once he saw me becoming more and more independent, he realized that at any moment I could pick up and leave, so he used his greatest weapon: fear. He gripped a hold of me, pinned me to the wall, and stared me in the eyes as he reminded me, "If you even dream about leaving me, I would come in your dream and kill you and your entire family."

I believed him, even though all my family were in the States. I guess he figured he scared the dodo out of me so even if he allowed me to visit my family, I would come running back like a little puppy who does not know anything about good treatment. Therefore, I would visit my family every summer with the intention of staying for six weeks. However, only after two weeks, he would call and say I must come home. Like an idiot, I went running back into the arms of defeat and doom. My family would say to me, "Every time you go to Nassau and come back, it gets worse for you."

He would accuse me of having a man in the States. Seriously, if I had a man in the States, do you think I would be coming back to this hellhole? Definitely not! He said that my family was no good and had no respect for our marriage. Is he serious? The only person who does not respect our marriage is him. He is the one who was beating on me like a raggedy punching bag in a gym. The only thing I had to call my own was my children. I wanted more for myself and for my children. So I started saving some money.

I told him I was saving my money to buy a car. We had a car, but it was his car. He would only lend me his car when he wanted to. Sometimes I would wait to go to church, and he would not come home in time for me to go. His actions were intentional.

His thing was, no woman was going to rule him and tell him what to do! I remember one Sunday morning, the children and I wanted to go to church, and he made it clear that we were not using his car. Pastor Sweeting, our pastor, came to pick us up in his truck. The children had to sit on the back of the truck while I sat in the front with the baby in my lap. Some Sunday nights, I would take the kids, and other times I would leave them home by themselves. If I did not have a ride, his sister Loretta would leave from Farrington Road and come to Carmichael Road to pick me up. It was a struggle and a journey, but I needed a way of escape from the madness.

CHAPTER 8

MY JOURNEY CONTINUES/ WIFE'S DENIAL

And he will be a wild man; his hand will be against every man, and every man's hand against him; and he shall dwell in the presence of all his brethren."

—Genesis 16:12

Remember, after our eighth child, we got another house that was under construction. Well, at baby number ten, we were still under construction, just like our marriage. Erwin went back to the bank many times and got a loan to finish the house and never did. I would cry and pray day and night, asking God to help me because by this time, I had eight living children and I saw no way out of the marriage. I saw no progress, no success; it was just a merry-go-round.

I continued to work at the drive-in theater. Debbie at the time was seventeen years old. Sandra, my sister, was about to have a baby. She asked if Debbie could come and stay with her, and she would send her to school. Surprisingly, Erwin agreed. So I packed her suitcase and sent her to Miami to live with Sandra. I breathed a sigh of relief. I knew this was only God! One of our children was out of the fire and into a better place. However, the abuse continued.

The events I am about to tell you I will never forget. The memory is as fresh in my mind as it was the night it happened.

I had just come home from work, and I had Erwin's car. He was not home. So I decided to go to the club to pick him up. When I asked for him at the club, his friends said he left. I went back home and locked the door. The children, Bernie being the oldest at home at the time, said, "Mommy, Daddy was here, and he is drunk. He said he didn't know where you were, and he went out to the club to look for you."

While she was yet speaking, Erwin came banging on the door. I looked through the window; there was fire in his eyes.

Bernie said, "No, Mommy, don't open the door."

My spirit left my body for a split second and watched me tremble in fear. I went toward the door like I was going to open it, only to put the other lock on it. Oh my Lord, why did I try that?

He said, "Woman, I am going to *kill* you tonight!"

I heard Bernie say, "Run, Mommy, run!"

At that moment, I knew my life depended on whether I ran or stood still. I could not stand against this beast that was about to take my life, but I knew God was not going to allow me to be slaughtered. His son was already the Lamb that was slaughtered for me. Erwin was still pounding on the door. It sounded as if he had a sledgehammer in his hand. I swore that door was going to cave in before I escaped. My spirit came back into my body, and I ran through the back door across to the neighbor's house. If a gold medal was given out that night for the fastest runner, I would have the medal and the trophy.

As I ran toward the neighbor's house, I could hear Erwin cussing me out. He was shouting, "You bad excuse for a wife! I don't know why I married you. You can't cook food fit enough for a dog to eat. Where you been, woman? You slut! Who you been sleeping with? I am going to f—— you up tonight."

I thank God for my daughter. Through all this, Bernie managed to keep a steady head. She called Lionel, her uncle, her dad's brother, and told him what was happening. He told Bernie to tell me to stay across at the neighbor's until he got there for me.

Bernie jumped through the window and came across to the neighbor's house to tell me what he said. Shortly afterward, Lionel arrived to pick me up. I was instructed to jump in the back passenger seat as soon as he came through. He reversed through the corner so he would have a good head start. As soon as I got in the car, Lionel pulled off, but Erwin was right behind him on his bumper. Erwin then overtook Lionel and cut across in front of him. Lionel had to stop. Then Erwin jumped out of his car, came to Lionel's car, pulled open the passenger door where I was sitting, pulled me out of the car on the road, and started beating me again across my head. My body wiggled on the road as I screamed, "Lionel, don't let Erwin kill me. Please, Lionel. Oh God, my children! If I die tonight, what will happen to them? Please help me, please!"

Somehow Lionel grabbed Erwin off me and told me to run around to the other side of the car, which I did. I jumped into the car. Sherry, Lionel's wife, locked the car door. We started off again toward Lionel's house.

Lionel was driving as fast as he could go.

He used his car phone to call his house to tell Barry, his friend, to open the door because he was bringing me. He also told him that as soon as I ran inside, to lock the door and not let Erwin in. By this time, Lionel was near his house. Erwin was right on his bumper. As soon as we reached the house, I jumped out the car and ran in the house. Erwin ran through the door, knocked Barry down, ran after me in the room, and started beating me again.

"You f—— b——! Did you think you could get away from me? You are my b——."

This time he was hitting me like two men fighting to the kill. The only problem was, I couldn't fight back.

I screamed, "Lionel, don't let Erwin kill me." With my last little bit of breath, I cried, "Lionel, please do not let Erwin kill me." I looked at Erwin punching me and shouting at me, and I cried, "Erwin, please, please stop! What have I done so wrong for you to be beating me like this?"

No matter how much I pleaded, he did not stop. It seemed as if the more I pleaded, the more he hit me and the harder the blows got.

Lionel came into the room; he could not find me because the light was off. After a few minutes, he grabbed Erwin and calmed him down. "What is wrong with you?" he said. Next, Lionel told me to run in his room. I did, and Sherry locked the door. I stayed the night there.

CHAPTER 9

MY JOURNEY IS ABOUT TO CHANGE

The God of my rock; in him will I trust:
he is my shield, and the horn of my
salvation, my high tower, and my refuge, my
saviour; thou savest me from violence.

—2 Samuel 22:3

The next day Sherry took me to her mother's house to stay. Why didn't I go to the police station or the hospital for medical attention? *Fear*! Fear will cause you to make decisions that are not in your best interest. If I had reported the abuse and he was locked up, I knew I was dead as soon as he was released. Although I was safe, my mind was not at rest. At this point, I was a disaster. I had no self-esteem. However, I knew I had to get out if I wanted to live to see my children grow up and become somebody in life. I also wanted to live to see my grandchildren. Therefore, I worked fast.

I knew Erwin had to go to work, so when he left home, I called the children and told them not to tell their dad they spoke to me. Bernie was the spokesperson. I told her I was leaving and going to Miami, and I was taking them with me. I instructed her to go in my drawer and take out all the passports and put them under her bed, but she must be quiet about it. That very next day, their dad came home and went in the drawer, took out the old passports, and locked them up in the back trunk of his car. He did not know Bernie had put the new ones away already. Bernie informed me that their passports needed visas. Therefore, I called Mel; after all, she owed me a favor. If I had not listened to her and had sex with Erwin in the first place, I would not be in this mess. I told Mel I needed visas for my children's passports. She knew someone at the visa office. She told me who to go to. I told Bernie to take the city bus downtown to the passport office and take the passports to have them stamped. During the next few days, their dad came home and questioned them about speaking to me. Every time he asked them if they spoke to me, they would say no. He would say to them, "Your mother left and went to Miami." They played along with him and acted as if he was right because they knew the truth.

It's time to make my getaway. I asked Sherry if she could take me to the airport. She said yes. I called Bernie and instructed her to pack the two suitcases with their clothes and put them under the bed with their passports in them. Sherry came and picked me up first. Next, we drove to the house to pick up the children. Once we arrived at the house, the children ran in the back of the truck which had a top on it so no one can see who was inside. Sherry drove us to the airport over on Paradise Island. I was so scared, my heart was pounding. I was certain Erwin knew we were trying to escape, and he was at the airport waiting for us. When we jumped out of the truck, Sherry pulled off as fast as she could. I went to the counter with my seven children to purchase our tickets. The clerk asked me if I wanted one-way tickets.

I said, "Can I?"

He said, "Yes, I will sell you one-way tickets," and he did.

That was God saying to me, "Go and don't look back."

We got our tickets and walked out toward the plane. We were still not safe; at any moment, Erwin could pop out of nowhere and drag us back to the house. As we walked toward the plane, I prayed, "Lord, please help us to get on this plane and into the air before Erwin realizes what is happening."

The flight attendant took our only two suitcases and put them in the back of the plane. Then he came and told us to get in; he put Erwin in my lap and buckled us in. There were only enough seats for seven of us. Debbie was not there, and Erwin was in my lap. As I look back to that day, I realize that God had everything set in place for me. There is no way in this world a nonresident can travel to the United States without a return ticket. Furthermore, what are the chances of getting on a flight with only enough seats for my family and me, no one else. Just us! The flight attendant was also the pilot; he jumped in the aircraft and flew the plane. When the plane lifted, I remembered something Martin Luther King said, "Free at last, free at last, thank God almighty we are free at last."

CHAPTER 10

MY TRAVEL EXPERIENCES

Moreover of the children of the strangers that do sojourn among you, of them shall ye buy, and of their families that are with you, which they begat in your land: and they shall be your possession.

—Leviticus 25:45

When we arrived in Miami, I wanted to kneel and kiss the ground. I could not believe I finally did it. I left Erwin Johnson. I was in a mess, though. I had no self-worth. I felt like I could not do anything. I felt like I was a failure. How could I subject my children to such abuse for such a long time? I was an unfit mother and wife. I was a bird who had been locked in a cage for years and was finally free. What was a prisoner to do in paradise? When I looked at my children, my heart filled with joy. Oh my God, the children were so happy and so relieved. They could not wait to tell my mom what happened.

We settled down that night. The very next day, my brother took me and the kids and got them the papers for school and shots so they could start school right away—no time wasted. My mother was a member of Revival Tabernacle Church, and she invited me to go with her that Sunday. The pastor was Selwyn Scott. The message he preached was "Turn Your Stumbling Blocks into Stepping Stones." That message was for me. Pastor Scott prayed for me and my eight children, and we became members of that church. Pastor Scott has been a wonderful and caring spiritual father to me and my eight children.

The very next week, my husband started calling me, telling me to come back. He was sorry, he had changed, and it would never happen again. He said he was coming into Miami in a couple of weeks; he wanted to see the children and me. I agreed and went to the hotel and saw him. However, Lionel was there. He begged, he pleaded, and he cried for me to come back. Yes, I thought he meant it. The very next day, I left and went to Nassau with him and took the two younger ones, Nicholas and Erwin. Why? Because I felt sorry for him, and I thought he needed me.

I was crazy to think such a thing. When I arrived in Nassau, I went to see his mother, who told me Erwin was going crazy over losing me and the children. "He would come by me every day and say Shelia is coming tomorrow," she exclaimed. Only to his surprise, no Shelia came. I got a job at the beauty salon as a receptionist. Shortly afterward, I found out there was a woman who was pregnant with his child. I found out where her mother worked and went to the school where her mom worked and told her mother to tell her daughter to leave my husband alone. She said her daughter was grown and could date any man she wanted to.

The very next day, I got a call from Ms. Lady, the woman who was pregnant by my husband. My husband told her where I was working. Her message to me was to leave her mother out of this. She had my husband, and she was going to keep him.

If I wanted him, I would not have left him and go to the States. I hung up the phone and started crying. The girls at the salon wanted to go beat her up for me. That wasn't necessary. I got what I deserved. God made a way of escape for me, and I went back to the mess.

As time went on, Erwin began talking so bad to me. He did not hit me, but he treated me so badly. I knew I made a big mistake in coming back. I continued to work. One year passed, and it was time for Bernie to graduate, so I planned to go to Bernie's graduation. Weeks before I was ready to leave, there was a holiday. So Icelyn, his younger sister, and I went to the beach and took the children. When we got there, we saw his car. Icelyn left me in the car to wait for Erwin.

Shortly afterward, he came walking with two women and some children. He identified me by saying, "That's my wife."

The woman, I found out afterward, was Ms. Lady. She began backing away. He said, "No, Ms. Lady, you come. I brought you out here, and I am taking you back." I don't know how she got here. He told them to jump in the car. I jumped in the car with Nicholas and Erwin in the front seat sitting in my lap. We drove away from the beach, only to stop because Erwin asked Ms. Lady if she wanted to dance. She said yes. They jumped out of the car and went dancing for a long time.

I sat in the car with Nicholas and Erwin. I was feeling like trash, not knowing what to do. Finally, they came back. Erwin drove Ms. Lady right up to her house. Her mother and family kept looking because I was in the front and Ms. Lady was in the back. It did not make any sense. This was the man who told me to come back home because he had changed and he missed me so much, yet he had another woman satisfying his desires.

Well, he drove back to the house. When we got home, I asked him, "Erwin, what are you going to do?"

He said to me, his wife, "I am with Ms. Lady. I am not going to leave her, and you can do what the f—— you want to do."

Oh my God, I almost fainted. I called my mother in Miami. I said, "I am coming. Erwin told me I can do what the f—— I want to do. I am coming."

She said, "Okay, don't tell him you are going to leave him because he may try to hurt you. Tell him you are coming for a trip."

I went to his mother's house and told her what he said. I then told her I was leaving.

His mother confronted him about it. He replied that this was his life and he would do as he chooses. She replied, "Don't come back to me when Shelia leaves again." I was due for a one-week vacation on my job in three weeks. I could not wait until then. I went to my boss and told him, "I have to leave. I need an early vacation."

He paid me, I packed stuff for my two kids, Nicholas and Erwin, and left. Erwin drove me to the airport. I told him I would be back in a couple of weeks, knowing that was not true. I said bye and left.

CHAPTER 11

IF SOMEONE CAN DEFINE YOU, THEY CAN CONFINE YOU

"Therefore, behold, the days come," saith the Lord, "that I will send unto him wanderers, that shall cause him to wander, and shall empty his vessels, and break their bottles."

—Jeremiah 48:12

After I arrived back in Miami, I realized I was not supposed to go back. God had given me one-way tickets to go and never look back. Afterward, I settled in Miami as best as I could with eight children. They were all split between my brothers and sisters. I had no say, but I just went along with what help I could get. When they realized I was serious, they started filing the papers for me and the children again so that we could become permanent residents. Shortly after two weeks, the calls from Erwin started again, telling me to come and asking me to forgive him. I thank God there was water between us because if there wasn't, I would have gone back again because his strong hold over my mind was not broken. I had no money, no career, and no degree. I started working in people's homes, cleaning their houses and getting paid cash. There were some rough days. My family did the best they could, and I thank God for all their help.

For the next two years, I worked whenever I could find work. My kids went to school, and I encouraged them to learn as much as they could. Not long after I settled in Miami, I met a nice man. We all thought he was godsent, but God never wants us to compromise. He helped with his money and his time, but it cost me.

He gave me money, and I had to give him sex. It was not what I was used to, but everybody was doing it, so it looked okay. Life served me lemons, I made lemonade. As time went on, in two years, I got my green card, with just four of the kids: Debbie, Bernie, Nicholas, and Erwin. The attorney suggested it was best to do it that way because they may not grant it with all eight of the kids. Then I had to wait for six months and go to Nassau and file for the rest of the kids, which was easy. They got it without any problem.

As time went on, the kids were growing up. I got a better job working at UPS; I also worked at the school part-time and had a few weekend jobs.

So I decided it was time for me to move into my own apartment. After much conviction by the Holy Spirit, I ended the relationship with that man. I want to live a moral Christian life. So I moved into my own apartment with Edwin, Shay, Nicholas, and Erwin. Debbie and Bernie had moved into their own apartment while Margarita and Theresa were in college. I tried to do it on my own without counting the cost. Shortly afterward, I went out one morning to take the kids to school, and my car was gone—repossessed. A friend named Lala Johnson helped me to get my car back. Shortly afterward, I was evicted.

That was something I had never experienced or seen happen to anyone before. One white man and two black men came.

The white man said, "We came to put you out."

They threw all my stuff outside. I was on the second floor. Bed, pots, shoes—everything was thrown out, and to make matters worse, it started to rain. As I gathered my things, Langston, my cousin, came and put my things in his truck and took me to my daughter's apartment. Just when I thought it couldn't get any worse, one of them asked me, "Mommy, how long are you going to stay here?"

My answer was, "As soon as I can find a place, I will be out."

During the time I was there, I slept on the couch, and my kids slept on the floor. One day I was so tired, I went and slept in my daughter's bed, and she came in and said, "Mommy, I was hoping you weren't in my bed because I want to go lie down and sleep." The bed was a double bed, big enough for both of us, but I said, "Okay, I will get up," and I did. She closed her door behind me as I left; oh, how that hurt!

Shortly afterward, within about two weeks, we moved out to Langston's apartment on 135th Street. It was a one-bedroom apartment for $250 a month. I was working two jobs, so I was able to pay the rent. We moved in, and the area was not good, but it was the best I could afford at that time. I had to work at twelve midnight, so I left Edwin in the house with Shay, Nicholas, and Erwin. All I could do was pray. I remember one night I was getting ready to go to work around 11:00 p.m., and there were so many termites in the place that if you opened your mouth, they would fly in.

I told Shay to call their older sisters and ask them if they can come and sleep over at their apartment while I go to work. Her sister wanted to know why they could not stay at their own place; after all, it was only termites. After begging her to let them come, she finally said yes. I dropped them off that night on my way to work and picked them up early the next morning after I got off work. I stayed in the termite-infested apartment for a couple of years. I found out Debbie and Bernie were moving out of their townhouse apartment, so I decided to rent it for me and the kids.

We moved in. That was much better than where we were. The rent was $5,000. By this time, Edwin was ready to go to college, and by the way,

Theresa got pregnant and had to come home from college. She stayed with Debbie and Bernie until she had the baby, a handsome baby boy she named Christopher. She and Chris's dad stayed in Miami for a while, then they decided to leave Chris with Fran and Earl and go back to college and finish their last two years. Well, the following year, Margarita got pregnant and moved in with me, which was a struggle for me. Margarita, her baby, Shay, Edwin, Nicholas, and Erwin were all living in a one-and-a-half-bath, two-bedroom townhouse apartment. I was the only one working two jobs. It was tough making ends meet. Within two years, Edwin went off to college in Alabama. Margarita moved out and got married to Paul. Theresa moved back home because she dropped out of college.

I continued working two jobs, and then I started to do Mary Kay. For the first time, I felt like I was doing something for myself that I liked to do. It was great. It built up my self-esteem and motivated me to believe in myself. I was doing fine. Shay graduated from high school, Nicholas and Erwin were in football, and things were looking better and brighter.

CHAPTER 12

DISAPPOINTMENTS ARE NOT COINCIDENCES—THEY ARE GOD-INCIDENCES

That which was torn of beasts I brought not unto thee; I bare the loss of it; of my hand didst thou require it, whether stolen by day, or stolen by night.

—Genesis 31:39

Then I got married to my husband at that time, "macho man." Shortly after that, I quit UPS thinking I could depend on my husband—wrong, wrong, wrong, bad move. I quit UPS to do Mary Kay full time. Shortly after two years in the marriage, my current husband had an affair. I lost my Mary Kay business. I was back at square one with no income. My husband wanted to stay, but I asked him to leave. I could not travel that road again. I moved out of the apartment myself. I had no income, and I could not pay for anything. Bernie had gotten married to Reginald, and Debbie was living with Bernie and Reginald with her baby, Dontae. Once again I was homeless, so Shay, Nicholas, Erwin and I moved in with them. We stayed there for about a year until I moved out and went back to my husband at that time, who was living in an efficiency. Nicholas and Erwin moved in with my friend Marie. Shortly, Edwin came back home; he had dropped out of college. He moved in with Marie also. After staying there for about one year, I moved out and went and lived with Shay and Theresa. By this time, Theresa was pregnant with her daughter, Paris. We stayed in the apartment for about one year. I finally got a job, working at the school part time. Theresa, Shay, Nicholas, Erwin, Paris the baby, and I decided to move into a bigger place. I got divorced. From there, I bought a used car. Struggling along, I managed to get out of depression with lots of prayer. I prayed day and night, and I cried day and night, "God, why can't I get a breakthrough? I have heard and read about people You have set free, and here I am serving You and still living in bondage."

Finally, I went back to the Bahamas to visit my mother-in-law, "Mama," who was very sick. I stayed at her house. By this time, Erwin, my ex-husband and the father of my eight children, had moved Ms. Lady into the house. She was sleeping in my bed, on my sheets. Her children were sleeping in my children's bed and wearing their clothes.

We left everything in the house and took only as much as could fit in two suitcases. Almost everything in the house was bought by my family. Shortly afterward, my mother-in-law died. I went to the funeral. Ms. Lady was there.

Thelma, my now-deceased cousin, approached her and told her what she did was wrong. "You took a father from his eight children."

Ms. Lady said, "If I could, I would change it."

I guess she was now experiencing what I went through. I used this opportunity to ask Erwin to help me with the children. He said he did not tell me to go to the States.

If I wanted help, I had to come back to Nassau. He was not going to help me as long as I was over in the United States. He never helped me with the children. I came back from the funeral only to find out that Theresa had married, and she and Shay had given up the apartment. I had nowhere to stay, again! Nicholas and Erwin left, wondering again where they were going to stay. At this time, I wanted to go somewhere and die. I came back and moved in with my daughter Margarita and her husband, Richard. They had two daughters, Ayesha and baby Aria. After about a year, Nicholas went off to college. He went to Florida Agricultural and Mechanical University. So Erwin and I stayed with Margarita and her family.

We stayed there until Shay got her own place and invited Erwin and I to come and stay with her. Shortly afterward, Erwin graduated and went off to college in Tennessee. That did not last very long.

After one year, he came back home and said college was not for him. He moved back in with Shay and me, which only lasted for about nine months. He was drafted into the armed services and went to join the Marines. Thank God! Something was finally working out.

Nicholas, on the other hand, after two years in college, got in trouble with the law, and that went on for about ten years. As I am writing this, it is still ongoing. Well, I finally got $20,000 from the property my ex-husband, Erwin, sold in the Bahamas. I brought it back, paid $5,000 to an attorney to keep Nicholas from going to jail, paid $5,000 down payment on the condo I had, and paid another $500 to bail Nick out of jail over and over again. I also lost $5,000 when the market crashed. Could it get any worse? I finally got a financial breakthrough, and it flew out of my hand like water.

CHAPTER 13

THIS IS GOD'S FAVOR, GOD HAS THE MASTER PLAN

The secret things belong unto the Lord our God: but those things which are revealed belong unto us and to our children forever, that we may do all the words of this law.

—Deuteronomy 29:29

By 2000, Nick has finally got himself together and out of trouble, thank God. Finally I got a full time para-professional position, and the opportunity came for me to go to college—hallelujah. In 2002, I enrolled in Florida Memorial University as a full time student majoring in elementary education and continued until 2006, spending four years in college. Working full time and going to school full time was a challenge, but I made it. I was a junior in college and felt good about my accomplishments. I owned my own Condo, and I was single and going to college. I thank God for my niece Vanteria, who helped me through many difficult times during my college experience.

After she left and went back to the Bahamas, I bumped my head. Yes, I did. My second husband, my husband at that time, who cheated on me, asked me to marry him after I had been divorced from him for ten years. I said yes. You can say maybe it was out of loneliness on my part, or the thought that I could not make it without a man. We had some good times for a few years, but then the marriage seemed like a dead end. I started to go into a state of depression, and I dropped out of college. I lost my condo and moved in with him. He had owned a one-bedroom condo, so we moved there. The marriage only lasted six years, from 2006 to 2012. I divorced him, moved out, got my own apartment, and enrolled back in college in 2014. Vanteria was now married and living in Miami. She encouraged me to finish my degree. There were many nights she stayed with me, helping me, to make sure I did not give up. Her husband always teased her by saying she was in the delivery room having her youngest son and helping me edit my paper over the phone. However, it paid off. I finished in 2016, graduated, and got my bachelor's degree in elementary education/ English for Speakers of Other Languages (ESOL). At sixty-seven years young, I am still working as a full time paraprofessional. The vision I had of being a school teacher, well, it's not going to happen anymore. I have now focused my vision on having a women's ministry to share my testimony and to teach women how to avoid the pitfalls of an abusive marriage, helping other women for the glory of God. As for my ex-husband, the father of my eight children, he is still residing in the Bahamas. He has remarried and has five children with his present wife, and my second ex-husband My husband at that time "Macho Man" is residing in Florida. But my most precious jewels are my eight children, who I love dearly. They have given me seventeen grandchildren, whom I love very much. God has been gracious and blessed them to be successful.

Through all of this, I never knew how my children were affected. I was so focused on the pain I went through that I thought it was only me. I thought I was shielding them by taking all the abuse. However, one day I thought to ask them for their side of the story. This is a little bit of my children's stories and what they went through, beginning with the oldest one in the order they were born.

CHAPTER 14

MY CHILDREN'S JOURNEY AND HOW THEY SURVIVED

Out of the mouth of babes and sucklings hast thou ordained strength because of thine enemies, that thou mightest still the enemy and the avenger.

—Psalm 8:2

My first child is Deborah, a school principal, and this is her story:

For as long as I could remember, I was doing housework, whether it was doing the dishes, washing clothes, sweeping, mopping, or taking care of my younger siblings. I was always doing something. I guess that's kind of the way it works when you're the oldest of eight children, even more so when the first four children are all one year apart. It forces the oldest sibling to grow up quickly. I don't remember much about being a toddler. I can only imagine that I was quiet and did what I was told. I do remember walking from nursery school when I was about four years old and walking with my sister and cousins from Chipping Ham to Farrington Road passing the graveyard and what appeared to be a ditch, where we all believed an old, scary man lived. When we approached the ditch, we would run with fear for our lives.

Another event that stood out the most to me was when I was about seven or eight years old. We were still living in Farrington Road, and I remember standing outside, passing Mommy the clothes as she hung them on the line. It was just me and my mom. I remembered the cold silence that made my heart ache so deeply. I thought to myself, *Why she won't talk to me? Did I do something wrong?* I desperately wanted to have a mother-daughter relationship; I wanted to feel a connection, to feel loved. On occasion, a neighbor would pass by and chat for a minute, then it would go back to silence. Once Auntie B stopped by and announced, "Boy, she almost as big as you." I didn't know it back then, but she was referring to my butt. At that time, I did not realize the pain my mom was going through; it had nothing to do with me.

Then came Oakes Field Primary School, where I attended from grades 1 to 6. I remember one day, on my way to school, I stopped by Uncle Eddie's shop and told him that Mommy said for him to give me a book and some crayons and she would pay him later. It was a lie, I guess I needed supplies for school, but it was better than stealing. Oakes Field Primary School provided a positive educational experience. I excelled in language arts and reading. I especially loved reading. I would read aloud in class and read to my sisters at home. Fairy tales were my favorite because they provided an outlet, an escape from reality, an opportunity to dream about a happily ever after.

I excelled in spelling as well; in fact, I was one of three top spellers in my class and would always receive 100 percent on my weekly spelling tests. My results, along with the results of two other students, would be posted for all to see. What a boost to my self-esteem, my ego, and my self-confidence that was. I felt smart! Imagine the blow to my self-esteem when at the age of ten in the sixth grade, I failed the entrance exam for Saint Augustine's College.

That experience haunted me for many years; it crippled me. I was devastated, and

I developed feelings of insecurity, incompetence, and fear; I didn't feel so smart anymore. So here I am in middle school. I didn't feel smart, and I didn't feel pretty. Everywhere we went, Bernie was immediately recognized as beautiful, Theresa was pretty, and Margarita was too busy crying, so no one really noticed her. I was the dark one with the big nose, and when my friends would see my sisters, they would say, "What happened to you?"

I was fifteen when the last child was born. Bernie and I were angry because there was another child to take care of, another diaper to change and wash. At that age, I had had enough of dirty diapers. But one look at that beautiful baby and we didn't want to put him down. We wanted to hold him, bathe him, comb his hair, and put it in a ponytail; he was our baby. One night while watching him, he would not stop crying, so we fed him and fed him some more. What were two kids to do? We didn't know any better! Shortly thereafter, he began throwing up; needless to say, we had fed him too much.

I didn't have much of a childhood. I didn't experience the joys of coming from a loving home. However, I learned how to cook, clean, and take care of children, and I also learned how to read my Bible and pray. Because of the faithfulness of our mother, we would gather each morning around her bed to pray. She taught us the Lord's Prayer, the Twenty-Third Psalm, and Psalm 121. We spent every Sunday in church—almost all day, morning and night, and then there were weeknight services.

Church, prayer, and praise—God was the one constant in my life. Because I knew how to call on the name of Jesus, He delivered me from a potential rape. The relationship that I developed with Christ as a child continues to sustain me through my adult life. Thank you, Mom, for introducing me to Jesus; because of Him, I no longer have a spirit of fear, but of power, love and a sound mind. I am more than a conqueror; I am an overcomer by the blood of the Lamb and the Word of my testimony.

My second child is Bernadette, District Director, Title 1 Programs, and this is her story.

My earliest recollection is when I was around four or five years old. You have to first understand that I was born several weeks premature (I was approximately 3.5 to 4 pounds at birth), and I had a deep raspy voice that was in direct contrast to my tiny frame. I was born one year and three months after my parents' oldest child and eleven months before their third child. It is also important to note that their fourth child was born eleven months after the third child as well. So at the time of this incident, there were at least four children under the age of five, and my mom was probably pregnant.

We went to church every time the church doors opened, and on this particular afternoon, we were getting ready to go to a program at our church. I remember sitting on the floor of our very small house, trying to put on my socks that were two or three sizes too big. Every time I tried to fold the foot of the sock over to put my foot in my shoe, a part of the sock hung out of my shoe. I remember looking around at the adults who were there: my mom, the neighbor's daughter who came by to help my mom with the younger kids, and other adults in the house. Well, every time someone walked by me, I cried out for help with putting on my socks and shoes properly.

I sat there for a while, but no one stopped to help me. I am not sure how long I sat there crying and trying to fix my socks in my shoes, but I remember hearing someone say, "We are leaving in a few minutes. Whoever is not ready they are going to get left behind."

At that point, I recall thinking, *I have to help myself. I cannot depend on anyone to help me, and I have to help myself.* I remember thinking, *I am going to do this, and I am going to fix this for myself.*

I did it; I was so proud of myself. I realized that if I put my mind to it, I could accomplish anything. For some reason, that particular incident helped to shape the person I am today. I don't sit around waiting for anyone to help me. If I need something, I go out and get it for myself. It has also shaped the way I look at others because I believe you should first try to help yourself before reaching out for help from others.

CHAPTER 15

BIRTH ORDER AND THE THIRD CHILD

I will say to the north, "Give up;" and to the south, "Keep not back: bring my sons from far, and my daughters from the ends of the earth."

—Isaiah 43:6

My third child is Margarita, a school teacher, and this is her story:

I'm not sure what to write. My growing up as one of the Johnson clan was just a small part of my life. To be honest, I can't remember anything in detail other than the fact that I cried all the time and that I was always hot and my skin itched all the time. Most of the memories of my younger years are kind of hazy, just glimpses of different experiences.

I was born eleven months after my second sister on July 31 or August 30. I'm not sure which is correct because my birth certificate says July, but my passport says August. Until the age of fourteen, I have celebrated my birthday on August 30. However, my birth certificate revealed that my birthday was in July. My mom disputes the birth certificate, but until she can prove it is incorrect, I will celebrate my birthday in July. Also, just as a note, my birth name is Mary Margarita, but no one was allowed to call me by my first name because my father was not very fond of my mother's mom, whose name was also Mary. So I was always called Margarita, which was my father's mother's name.

One memory in particular that comes to mind is the Christmas play at Independence Drive Church of God. My sisters and brother, Edwin, who was the only boy at the time, always participated in the Christmas play. This was a big highlight for my family because my older sisters Debbie and Bernie were always the angels, along with all the other older girls in the church. They would run in a circle around the inside of the church singing:

> Angels from the realms of glory,
> reign your flight all over the earth;

He who sang redemption story
now proclaims the Messiah's birth.
Come and worship; come and
worship,
Worship Christ the Lord our
newborn king.

At the end of the Christmas production, my brother played the part of an old man dressed in a tuxedo and a top hat. He would say this poem that made everyone laugh:

Christmas is coming; the goose is
getting fat
Would you please put a penny in
the old man's hat?
If you haven't got a penny, a half
penny will do;
if you haven't got a half penny,
God bless you.

I can't remember what role I played, but I remember that it was a happy time.

Researcher Robert Plomin discovered that when it comes to how we look and how our brains work, we're usually pretty similar to our siblings. Yet when it comes to personality, even though we share similar genetic material and upbringings, brothers and sisters often can't be more different. He also states that tests done on siblings to measure personality demonstrated that siblings might as well be strangers. Similar studies revealed something else as well. Even if you and your sibling are vastly different, those who didn't grow up as only children are generally happier than their counterparts.

I'm realizing as an adult that I'm a lot different from both of my older sisters, and I don't have much in common with my two younger sisters.

Research says that siblings who are born first tend to have a substantial academic advantage. They outperform their younger siblings by the equivalent of having had an extra year of schooling and are more likely to score higher on an IQ test. There are several theories on why this is the case, the strongest being that older siblings spend time teaching their younger siblings, thereby reinforcing their own understanding of concepts and ideas. I believe this is true mainly because my older sister was always seen as the smart one. She went to a school for smart students, and she was always reading or memorizing something. Many times after church, she would pretend to be our teacher and go over our schoolwork. My second sister was always giving instructions; she was seen as the bossy know-it-all. However, my two younger sisters were the ones who I believe both my parents preferred. My sister Theresa was my dad's favorite, and my baby sister was my mom's favorite. Over the years, my dad had always said who was his favorite, but my mom has outwardly denied that she has a favorite child. However, studies have proven time and time again that this simply isn't the case.

As the middle daughter of five girls, I'm not at the top or bottom; I'm smack-dab in the middle. I never tried to mimic any of my sisters or follow in in their footsteps. I have tried to de-identify with all four of them. Over the course of my life, I have purposely attempted to be different from each of my sisters and stake out my own role in the Johnson family dynamics. While I have spent a lifetime with my seven siblings, getting to know every quirk, trait, and annoying habit that they have—Erwin and Nick especially—I often stop and think of the real impact that my sisters and brothers have on who I am and how I act.

Whether it's the order I was born into or all that good-natured love and concern or the bad-natured ribbing and teasing to which we subjected each other, I can honestly say that my siblings have had an intense and long-lasting effect on my life, influencing everything from the way I dress, what I eat, how I rear my children, and most importantly, how I interact with others. Coming to America was a pivotal point in my life. At the age of fifteen, I was catapulted into a new life and culture. Much of what I did in my life in the Bahamas was gone. There was no more hanging out with my siblings, spending time in the yard, and going to church on Sundays.

My fourth child is Theresa, CEO/owner of Legacy Private Care, LLC, and this is her story.

Ask any of the eight children, and you'd probably get eight very different perspectives about our life in the Bahamas. As for me, I've always felt very much loved, but this is entirely my perspective. My first memory—wow—was when I was about four years old, and I remember crying and waving goodbye from a window at the Princess Margaret Hospital as my family headed home without me. As a child, I was asthmatic, which led, to some degree, to me getting care and attention. In addition, I'm the fourth of eight children who are only separated by one year. Aftcr me, my brother Edwin falls almost three years behind. This meant I was the baby far longer than any of my siblings were, and this act positioned me to again receive extra care and attention that babies often get. As a child, I remember always having a hot breakfast before school, mostly cream of wheat but sometimes grits and eggs. My mom also prepared sandwiches for our lunch, which consisted of peanut butter and jelly, tuna salad, or my favorite, egg salad. At night, we always had supper; this was our meal after dinner. Supper consisted of tea and bread. The bread was homemade, baked by my dear mommy, and the tea wasn't tea at all but rather hot chocolate—Milo or Ovaltine, to be exact. Why we called it tea and bread is unclear.

Two fond memories about Mom and the girls come to mind:

1. I can recall a few Saturday mornings that my mom would shampoo and hot iron (we call straighten) her four older girls' hair. It was a long and tedious task as I look back on it, but oh, how we loved it.
2. I remember Mommy sitting on the kitchen floor, playing jackstones with us; I still love that game to this day. Her raising us taught lasting lessons. To say church was a huge part of our lives would be an understatement. Church was really our only outing, and there was a time when we went four to five times a week. If it was revival time, we went six to seven times a week. My mother never sent us but accompanied us. This was an undertaking solely all her own; my dad did not participate in this

> endeavor. We went to vacation Bible school almost every summer and could recite many verses from the Bible that often impressed our aunts and uncles.

As I reflect on the magnitude of what my mother dealt with on a daily basis and knowing what I now believe I do, I can say with all certainty that it was her *faith* that carried her through. In fact, fast-forward to present time and I recall my mom recently saying she was mostly numb during those years.

About my siblings and me:

We were affectionately known as "Debbie dem," which is interpreted as "Debbie and all of her sisters and brothers." We were the "dem."

We were taught manners early: the importance of please, thank you, good morning, good night, and so on. We were never allowed to call each other names, use profanity, or fight each other—things siblings generally do. That is not to say we didn't, but we were taught not to. My mom not only told us to pray, but she knelt at our bedsides and prayed with us. We were taught each morning as we woke and before doing anything else to kneel and pray. Then our beds had to be made, and afterward we brushed our teeth and washed our faces.

These are the very values I hold dear, and I have practiced them throughout the years. I've desperately tried to pass them along to my children with the hopes they'd do the same when they become parents. I believe despite everything and even with very different perspectives, my siblings and I are perhaps most thankful for the loving and supportive mother we have and the lasting values she has instilled in us.

About Mommy and me:

It was difficult to ever get a one-on-one with Mommy because she was split in eight different pieces, nine if you included my dad. However, because of my asthma, I wasn't able to be around when cleaning was done on Saturday. That meant I went to the laundromat—or as we called it, the wash house—with Mom. I was ever so happy to go. It was just Mommy and me. To this very day, I actually enjoy doing laundry, and I believe it's because I have such sweet memories of being with my mother.

Finally, to sum it all up, although we may not have had the fancy clothing or gifts and parties as other children did, it never bothered me. In fact, I never really noticed much of what we didn't have, and I attest that to the abundance of love bestowed upon us by my mother. This love far surpassed anything else. Of all the love and gifts she has given me over the years, I'm most grateful that she introduced me to Jesus, the greatest gift ever. My encourager, my inspiration, and my friend and confidant is my darling mother, Shelia.

CHAPTER 16

A TALE OF TRIUMPH OVER DIFFICULTIES

Even unto them will I give in mine house and within my walls a place and a name better than of sons and of daughters: I will give them an everlasting name, that shall not be cut off.

—Isaiah 56:5

My fifth child is Edwin. He is my first son, and he is a schoolteacher. This is his story:

Farrington Road in Rock Crusher is where my parents lived when I was born. We lived in a small house until it burned down. The family across the street had several youths, too, and the girls my age would come with me their house once or twice. I don't remember much about this house except that we had an outhouse. Maybe that's why I wet the bed so much, even as a bigger youth. Going to the outhouse at night was like a real-life haunted house experience. Nevertheless, living in Farrington Road was a cozy experience for me, especially because we were able to walk through an alley between some houses to get to our cousin's house.

When we moved to Carmichael Road, I was about four or five. I remember when we received a car loaded with gifts and items for the house from Uncle Van and Auntie Sandra in the States. I got a Big Wheel. That was so cool. I remember my favorite blue sneakers. When I got a little older, I got a bike. It was one of those bikes that never went flat because the tires were just hard rubber and had no inner tube. It had a bread-loaf seat, and I taught myself how to ride after many falls on the rocky road with lots of holes in it. I would ride past Lavinia, the Haitian lady who sold tomato paste, and up to the corner house store where they sold those red-and-yellow candies that I loved. I remember well our unfavorable socioeconomic status in the Bahamas, but also I remember the many fruit trees and plants in the yard. These are the list of the trees that I remember we had in our yard: cherry, plum, mango, sapodilla orange, sweet sop, coconut, orange, and breadfruit. There were also yams that grew below the ground. I can be described as the loner, the family member who was not here but near. Coming from a family with many siblings, it's not uncommon to experience the irony of being connected to many but less significantly to a certain degree. When being addressed by others, often I was called Erwin, or Nick, and conversely Erwin and Nick were sometimes called Edwin.

I remember hanging with Daddy, which was a privilege. Sometimes he would hang out at Golden Aisles Club, where he also was a bouncer. I remember growing up in the Bahamas and being out back, way behind the house, all by my lonesome self for hours during the summer. I really enjoyed exploring the terrain. Things even got exciting sometimes, and I might see a huge dog dash in front of my path. Other times I would be in the field across the street, catching bees in a bottle until one of them stung the heck out of me, then I was done.

The dilly tree and cherry trees also were exciting places because of the many times I got stung by wasps trying to pick those sweet fruits. I remember trying to cut grass in the front of the yard like I saw the Haitian man do and almost chopped my finger off. I remember jumping of the roof of the unfinished two-story building, busting my mouth when my knee hit my lip, and trying to flip backward in the bed and landing on my neck. Yeah, I thought I was going to die that day.

Then there was the time Debbie was chasing me around the house, and I ran right into the wall by my bedroom. I've got a scar on top of my head today because of that incident. Another time I remember getting held down and tickled by my older sisters until I cried. I remember getting a cut ass (a beating) by Mom, because I was trying to have sex with a girl in the living room while everybody was home. Yeah, I must have been possessed, but the cut ass delivered me.

I remember Shay getting old enough to hang with me around the house, but she always would get hurt when she hung with me. I guess it was my fault. I could have been a better big brother. On four separate occasions, Shay got herself seriously hurt while with me. One was the ruler she had in her mouth that had a jagged edge. I don't recall the details except she was chasing me and ran into a wall with the ruler in her mouth. Another time Shay was chasing me around the house outside at night. We ran and ran, and I knew she was not as fast so I expected her to be behind me, but it wasn't until I came back around to her, I saw what had occurred. Shay just sat there on the floor with a pitchfork in her foot. Somehow she ran into the pitchfork that was hidden in the grass. It went straight through her foot. I ran and got Daddy; he came and pulled it out of her foot.

I could go on and on about Shay and her calamities with me, from falling out the plum tree to getting hit in the face with a makeshift baseball bat. To be honest, I feel like I'm to blame for all of them. If she had not been with me, none of those events would have occurred. All were my fault except when Daddy whipped her and me for laughing and giggling on the couch while he was talking to a guest at the house. I actually wasn't trying to annoy Daddy, but Shay seemed to have little regard.

That was one of the only three times Daddy whipped me. The other times were causing the German shepherd to kill her puppies because I didn't feed her, and causing the chicken to die in the hot sun because I decided to do as I saw him do and catch a chicken by causing it to go into a trap that I had held up with a stick and a string. So I caught the chicken, but I then lifted it and went God knows where. The chicken was in the sun all day and died. When Daddy came home, the fun and games were over.

For some reason, even though I had many sisters, I always was alone at school. The preschool at the church was my first. I remember making a fool of myself and eating dirt to show off for the other kids. Yeah, and I had worms after that. My first public school was Carmichael Primary; it was about a half-mile walk. I remember my shirts' buttons were always broken, as if I was always in a fight. At times, school seemed like a war zone for me, but at times it was peaceful or just boring unless I was able to go outside in the back and try to hit the birds in the trees with a slingshot. Flipping in the sand with the other boys was always fun, too. One time, instead of going the street way home, I decide to go through the bushes, and it was like uncharted territory, with vines and rocky areas and areas that almost seemed impassable. When I finally made it home, it had to be close to dinnertime. In third or fourth grade, I went to CW Sawyer Primary School. It was a bigger school with more kids. The classes were set up so four classes were in one room. It seem very unproductive and noisy most of the time. Nevertheless, I thought I was smart. Interestingly enough, I don't recall my grades. I just recall answering lots of questions the teacher asked.

In that same big class, I was marginalized and ripped of my dignity by a fat teacher who decided she wanted to make an example of me. She told everyone to be quiet. I sat there, not thinking of trying to disrespect her or even thinking about her, and like a fourth grader would do, I decide to puff out my jaw. I guess she thought I was trying to make fun of her obesity and called me out. Off course, I was looking around like "What did I do?" She picked me up, pulled my pants down, and whipped me in front of the class. I forgave her fat ass, but I wish I could see her today to tell her how wrong she was for that.

When I mentioned it to my parents, I still got no justice, but I survived fourth grade and went to fifth and then sixth grade. In sixth grade, I was ten, and I would walk about three or four miles to the Super Value grocery store and pack bags after school. My cousin Andrew worked there. They called him "Saddest." I would go to the register when the hired boys were not there and bag customer groceries. Some of them scorned me while others respected me. They liked it when I would chose a customer who would probably take me on a mile or so journey to their house. That happened a few times.

One time a bag boy said to me, "Hey, why don't you see if they would hire you?" So I got my courage up and went up to the manager. He looked at me and said, "No, you are too young." I then got a glass eye, and just as I was walking out, the lady inside the office said something to him, and he said, "Okay." I was overjoyed, and every day after school, I would walk about three or four miles to work. At night when the store closed, we had to clean up. Each boy got an aisle or two. The aisle seem huge to my small frame, but I wanted to show and prove that I could hang with the big dogs, so I got it done.

Coming to work was the best part of my day, especially because of how I used to get picked on after school by a bigger youth. I told my cousin Andrew, whose nickname is "Saddest," and he told me to pick up a big rock and hit him with it. I also went with Mom sometimes when she worked at the drive-in movie theater. I somehow ended up in the room where the wheel to reel was. I'm sure it wasn't a good idea to do, but a guy who worked in there allowed me to change the hot pipes with a metal tong. He would leave, but before he did, he told me to just watch it for when it got small enough to change out and put a new one in. That was an awesome learning experience. Another tiring yet amazing experience was riding my bike all the way home from Super Value while Daddy rode beside me. That was about five miles or so.

I remember graduating from sixth grade at CW Sawyer and coming to the States that summer and being placed back in fifth grade. I didn't feel like I had a voice, but I knew I hated that. I wasn't held back a grade; I was put back two grades. When I voiced my opinion, nothing was done, so I graduated high school at nineteen even though I never failed a grade. I remember coming to the States on at least two occasions before having permanent residence and staying at Mary's house.

Mary was my mother's mother, and everyone called her Mary. Mary had a bright yellow house that could be spotted from a distance. There was one tree in the front yard, and it had a small orange sour-like fruit that we would pick and eat. Mary's house was an interesting place, with a special living room that was off-limits to us and hanging beads that separated the front room from the other, rare part of the house. Mary would make us bread and butter on occasions, but I don't recall much cooked food.

In 1980, Debbie graduated from high school and came to the United States to live and go to school. However, in 1982, we all also came to the States by way of a small plane that left from a small airport. This trip was different because it was an escape for Mom from Dad's abuse. Even though Dad would hit my mom, I myself had never once seen this happen. I don't know why I didn't see any abuse, but I know it did occur.

This could be what fueled a dissension between my sisters and me. I know some of it was typical sibling rivalry, but we didn't really bond. I remember having discussions when we had just recently come over, where

I tried to defend my dad but was reminded that his ways were not at all good. After arriving here to live, we were split up because there were eight children with my mom. My dad decided he was going to come and get us, which he did. My mom, Nicholas, and Erwin left with him.

Uncle Van and Uncle Mannie were furious, but they ended up going back anyway. It wasn't long after that they were on a plane heading back to the United States because of the same issue. Shay and I were also living back in the Bahamas during part of the first few years of coming to the States. There was a visa immigration issue, and we were stuck in the Bahamas, staying at Aunt Pat's house for several months. That was cleared up, and Mom came and got Shay and me.

When we first came to the States, Shay and I went to Parkway Elementary, and were both placed in fifth grade. I didn't know what was going on, and I had no voice to speak up for me concerning that situation. Our socioeconomic status was below the poverty line, and I myself also was dealing with typical teenage issues. Thus, life wasn't a bed of roses for me. Like with others areas in my life, I wish that I was a better person during that time.

Sandra, Van, and Winnie were very generous to my mother and her eight children.

Even though things were rough, we always had shelter, thanks to them. Growing up in Miami back then, boys actually wanted to be outside as much as they could. This allowed me to play street football, ride bikes, wrestle with the other boys, or just hang out at certain areas in the neighborhood. I even learned to swim in the lake behind Aunt Sandra's house. I will never forget that day because I almost drowned after wicked Kenny pushed me off the boat that we were playing on.

Up to this day, I believe that guy was really trying to kill me because he knew I couldn't swim. After being pushed off the boat in the deep area of the lake, I tried to grab on to the boat that floated farther away from me in the deeper area. I then went underwater and swam to the area I could stand up in. It was a traumatic experience, but I learned to swim that summer.

Just like a tree that may need to be propped up to help it grow straight instead off to one the side, I, too, needed that. A little guidance, I know, would have made a world of difference. Life to me during my early years in the United States was filled with sadness and no guidance. When I looked back at those days, even when I thought I was enjoying myself, I was just being a teenager trying to fit in. I was trying to fit in with the wrong crowd, and it caused me many problems in my young adult years.

Yes, I was able to go to parties at the skating rink or the local teen nightclub, but I gained absolutely nothing from those experiences except to stay clear when you see a guy getting kicked to sleep by a group of other guys. Another caveat I gained was to be aware of the prevailing racism by cops. This experience was also very traumatic, and it prompted a shift in paradigm for me and my perspective of cops. This incident occurred when I was fourteen or fifteen. A friend and I were at a skating rink in Broward County where Luke and the 2 Live Crew were supposed to be. My friend and I got dropped off and were supposed to call when we were to be picked up.

The skating rink closed early after a fight broke out. We stood in front of the skating rink, waiting, but were told we had to leave there, even though there were whites standing in front of the skating rink. After a while, it seemed as if all the blacks had left. My friend called his ride, and we waited. While waiting, cops approached us and told us we had to leave where we were standing, even after we told them we were waiting on our ride. That night, we were approached several times by different cops who told us to leave where we were. We ended up in the median and, of course, were told we had to leave there, too. The cops eventually got out and assaulted me. A big muscle-bound Caucasian police officer grabbed me and threw me against a tree, kicked my legs apart, and roughed me up. It was one of the experiences that fueled a dislike for Caucasians within me because it was evident that we were being profiled for no reason except because of our skin. Despite the many challenges and hardship, prayer was the key to our success. I remember being awakened by Mom to pray with the family early every morning. I'm certain the prayers Mom led us in were a major key, as God's mercy and race guided us all through the years.

CHAPTER 17

THE LAST GIRL AND HER SURVIVAL STORY

Yet, behold, therein shall be left a remnant that shall be brought forth, both sons and daughters: behold, they shall come forth unto you, and ye shall see their way and their doings: and ye shall be comforted concerning the evil that I have brought upon Jerusalem, even concerning all that I have brought upon it.

—Ezekiel 14:22

My sixth is Shay, and she is a vocational education instructor/guidance counselor, and this is her story:

I am currently an employee with Miami Dade Schools and have been employed for approximately sixteen years now; however, this journey and path here started over fifteen years ago at the age of sixteen. I started my vocational education in 1989 at Miami Lakes Vocational Tech School, where I was enrolled as a cosmetology student. I was considered a share time because I spent half of my school day at my high school, and the other half of my school day at Miami Lakes Tech (MLT). This path gave me an early start into what was to become a rewarding and exciting career. Approximately two years after entering beauty school at MLT in 1991, I not only graduated with a high school diploma but simultaneously graduated from vocational school. I diligently earned my certificate of completion and was qualified to take the state board examination. Immediately I sat for Florida Board, passed, and became a licensed professional at the age of seventeen. Thus, my Miami Lakes technical education has set the foundation for my career. Graduating from high school and becoming a licensed professional, I pursued an advanced education at Miami Dade Community College but later transferred to Florida International University, where I obtained my bachelor's degree in psychology. Subsequently while attending college as a full-time student and working in the salon as a full-time apprentice, I was able to learn my skills and quickly excelled as a private contractor, managing a small business.

After gaining thirteen years of experience in the cosmetology industry as a hairstylist and purposefully sharpening my craft as a beauty consultant, I felt the time had come to pursue other interests. My confidence as a young entrepreneur had grown, and my desire for growth became commonplace for me. Alternatively, it seemed that my childhood fear of not able to succeed had become the hallmark for my future success. In the fall trimester of 2000, I applied for a teaching position with Miami Dade County Public Schools. I was hired and began a teaching career as a substitute teacher and then as a part-time teacher at my old technical school Miami Lake Tech, MLT.

By the fall of 2001, I was hired as a full-time instructor in my dream career: teaching cosmetology at my old school, Miami Lakes Tech. Then just two years later in 2003, I completed additional advance education and training, with a teaching vocational education certification" at Florida International University (FIU). I then became certified with the Florida Department of Education. My duel career as an entrepreneur and now full-time vocational education instructor kept me extremely busy and quite active, from hair shows to job fairs.

Teaching cosmetology was even more rewarding than I imagined. I found it fulfilling to be able to give back to my community, paving a path for students in an area that I knew all so well. I was recognized and nominated twice by my colleagues as "ML Teacher of the year." It was a great honor. Yet still I had a desire to aspire for even more, and that drive to succeed became a burning flame. Thus, I went back to school to pursue degrees in guidance counseling. In December 2005, I graduated with honors from Nova Southeastern University (NSU) School of psychology, guidance, and counseling master's program.

In addition to my guidance, teaching, and vocational education, I have also volunteered as a hairstylist for Revlon, helping the less fortunate and participating in hair seminars, hair shows, and the like. In 2004, I sat as a judge in the VICA State Competition Florida skills and leadership conference, and I am currently a member of Antioch Missionary Baptist. I am now teaching at Miami Lakes Technical College, and I manage the school cosmetology salon. I continue to pursue numerous other ventures and exciting challenges on my journey to succeed. Yes, I have stumbled sometimes but always forward. Thus, my education and career path have all been orchestrated in such an amazing turn of events that all started at the age of sixteen when I enrolled as a student at Miami Lakes Technical Cosmetology School. I owe my success to God, my mom, a close-knit family, and an awakening childhood that has created a tenacious, keen, and strong individual.

CHAPTER 18

A MOTHER'S SACRIFICE: PRAYER CHANGES THINGS

The effectual fervent prayer of a righteous man availeth much.

—James 5:16

My seventh child is Nicholas, and he is a licensed plumber.

What I remember about being the seventh child out of eight is always having my older sisters do things for me. It always felt like, and still does at times, that I have help and support. I was too young to remember the time when we all lived in one house. I could only imagine how it was, just by knowing how our personalities are. I look at my sisters and brothers, and I can see two who are similar in their mannerisms and thought process. However, I don't see any of them as similar to me. Maybe I don't want to see it. Although we are all different and went through rough times together, I truly love all my brothers and sisters and will do anything they ask.

One of the great things I like to say when people ask me if I have any brothers or sisters is, "Yes, I do! I have five sisters and two brothers, all from the same parents," just to let people know my family isn't blended. I met a lady who also had eight children from the same man. It was amazing to see how jolly and high spirited she was. That is just how my mom is. One of my greatest joys is bringing a smile to my mom's face. My mother used to be so "island." What I mean by that is she was the typical island parent. She used to say all the island quotes. It was hard for me to understand some of it because I grew up here in the United States. The cultures are so different. It was hard adjusting to the American culture and trying to understand my culture of birth. One of my mom's quotes was, "When you have your hand in the lion's mouth, you have to take it out slow." The crazy thing is, I am an adult now, and I still don't know what that means. My mom was so used to saying these quotes that it was natural to her. She had already raised six other children on those quotes and her beliefs. I guess she believed they would work for me. The funny thing is, my mom doesn't say those quotes as much as she used to. I guess she has become more "Americanized."

In addition to getting used to her famous sayings, I also had many happy times with my mom. One of the happiest times I had with my mother was when I was in elementary or middle school. One of my drawings was picked to go to the fair, and I had to take a picture next to my drawing. I think it was during the school day. I remember getting dressed up and going with my mom to the fair downtown to take a picture next to my drawing. Even though she had work and we needed the money, she took the time off from work just to take me. She never realized how special that moment was.

While I was in middle school, I can remember my mom working two jobs. I didn't realize it at the time, but if she didn't work like that, we wouldn't have been able to live as well as we did. I remember times when my mom used to get off from work being tired so I would go to the car to help bring her bags into the house. Afterward, I would make her something to eat. It was not a gourmet meal, but she knew it was made with a lot of love. Once I got into high school, my mother still worked *two jobs*. Can you say *super woman*? Although she worked two jobs, she still took the time to get up and cook me and my younger brother breakfast. Although this only lasted until I was a sophomore, this was one of the moments I will always cherish.

Another time I remember is my mom having fish fry at our house on Fridays. This was when we lived in Miami Gardens. I remember family members coming over to eat, talk, and dance until late at night. I also remember my mom's famous carrot cake that she used to bake. I was the one who cleaned and cut the carrots up. Those were some great times!

After high school, I wanted to go off to college to get away from the family. I felt that I had enough of being around them. So I went off to college and didn't call or come home as much. My mother always called to check on me and always prayed on the phone with me no matter who was around. There were times when I had to put the phone on speaker, and whoever was in the room with me was included in the prayer. At first, I used to be a little embarrassed, but after a while, it became okay because my friends already knew she would pray. It was times when I would call because I knew my mom's prayer was the only thing that would fix my situation.

My mother always was able to tell if the girl I dated was right for me. She would tell me "my spirit doesn't feel right about her," or "She has a good spirit—I like her." The crazy thing is, ninety percent of the time, she was right.

There was a time period where I got into trouble around the same time every year. My mother would say, "It's a pattern. You need to break whatever it is that is causing this to happen." Yet no matter how many times it happened, my mother was right there. Each time I would have a court date, my mother was there. It used to hurt knowing she was in such a place because of me, but it gave me peace in my heart knowing she was there with me.

One of the most important times in my life was when I had to go in front of an immigration judge to rule on if I can stay in the United States or go back to the Bahamas forever. The cards were stacked against me, and nothing looked good for me. Yet my mother, my darling mother, stood in the gap for me one more time. She interceded on my behalf to the God whom she serves. The great God Jehovah who has never let her down. Although the outlook appeared hopeless, she was the only person who knew I would not be deported. My mother prayed me out of that situation. To God be the glory. After all

> the problems and setbacks, I finally graduated from college. After seeing all that I put my mother through and she was still by my side, my drive was to get my college diploma to make my mother proud.
>
> Now that I am older, I have noticed how much sacrifice my mother made just for me, her seventh child. I took it for granted when I was younger. I thought it was *normal* for every mother to treat and care for their children the way she did for me. I have conversations with friends who say they go weeks and months without talking to their mother. I cherish all the time I have with my mother, and that is why I thank God for her. I got a tattoo in honor of my mom's sacrifice for me. I want everyone to see it has praying hands with the inscription, "Thank God for Shelia." Her love and sacrifice made me appreciate the sacrifice Jesus made for us. It is a true demonstration of pure love. I know I would have never made it this far in life if it wasn't for God and my mother's prayers.

My eighth child is Erwin. He has his dad's first name. He is a United States Marine gunnery sergeant, and this is his story:

> When we think about people who have influence your life, most people think about great athletes like Michael Jordan,

Jesse Owens, and Jackie Joyner-Kersee. These great athletes have affected a lot of people lives in a positive way by helping them to accomplish dreams that they never thought were possible. When I think about the person who has had a significant influence in my life and has affected me in a positive way, I don't think about great athletes, inventors, or even celebrities.

If anyone was to spend a day with me, they would know there would be no question as to who this person is. She is small in body but mighty in words. She always has something motivating to say, and people listen. She is a mother of eight, who has traveled from another country, leaving a wife-beating husband behind. Life has not been easy for her, trying to raise eight children in a foreign country all alone. But because of her faith and trust in God, she never lost hope. She always believed that God will make a way, and He always did. She always had a positive attitude about life even when times were hard, and she didn't have money to pay her bills or put food on the table. In spite of it all, she always kept a positive attitude and a smile on her face.

She encouraged us to pray, read our Bible, go to church, and do well in school. Even though I didn't know then it was for my good, she would not let me hang out in the streets. She made me get into my books or go to church. Even though I am not the best student or the best child, I am not doing so badly, and I thank my mother for that. She does not smoke, she does not use profanity, and she never drinks alcohol, so I wasn't able to pick up any of the bad habits. More than anyone that I have ever known, my mother has the greatest influence in my life.

Through her strength, motivation, and encouragement when everyone wrote me off as a delinquent child, my mother was the one who saw the potential that was inside of me. She understood that the absence of a father and the desire to feel a part of something was the main reason for my actions. She believed that as long as she just kept showing me the right path, I would find my way. I remember that during my four years of high school football, the night before every game, she anointed my body from head to toe with olive oil and prayed over me. I believe that is the main reason why I never had a single injury. After I returned from an unsuccessful attempt at college, she made sure that I was doing something with my life.

The day I left for Marine Corps boot camp, even though she knew the Lord would protect me, I could tell she was scared that her baby boy was signing up to do one of the most dangerous jobs in the world. For the six duty stations I have been to so far, the one main person I know that will come and see me is my mom. Before I can even speak to her about coming to visit, she would have already been online, researching airline tickets.

At the age of thirty-six, married with three kids and an eighteen-year career with the United States Marine Corps, I can say to my mom, "*Job well done*!" Something that she always told me and that I would never forget is, "All it takes is all you got. Hold on to your dreams."

CHAPTER 19

EMPTY NEST: WHO IS THE *ME* LEFT BEHIND

And my people shall dwell in a peaceable habitation, and in sure dwellings, and in quiet resting places.

Isaiah 32:18

As for me and where I am now, I took an inventory of my life and realized that my eight children are all grown up, financially independent, and taking care of their families. The relationship between me and my girls has gotten better now that they have children of their own, and they understand motherhood. My relationship with the boys weren't as complicated as with the girls. However, I always loved my kids. I would have died for them if I had to.

Well, my nest was finally empty, and it was time for me to think about myself. As I took an inventory of my life, I realized I did not have a good marriage, having been divorced twice; nevertheless, I never gave up hope. I continued to pray and believed God. I did not want to be alone, and then it happened through a phone connection. We connected, not knowing what each other looked like. Jerry proposed to me over the phone. Was he crazy, or was I insane? This is how it happened

A Real Love Story: One to Die For!

It was October 18, 2014 at 10:30 a.m. on a Saturday; it seems like yesterday. We were on a telephone conference call, and the moderator was talking about soul mates and the importance of praying for a mate. On this telephone conference call, there were about five hundred-plus people from all over the United States. Anyone who wanted to be on that call had to have a fictitious name; therefore, my fictitious name was "Simply the Best." I responded to the moderator by saying I am praying for a husband, for a real man of God, a man who loves the Lord. I continued by saying I believe a man who loves the Lord will know how to love his wife. The Bible in Ephesians 5:28 says,

> Husbands, love your wives, even as Christ also loved the church, and gave himself for it; That he might sanctify and cleanse it with the washing of water by the word. That he might present it to himself a glorious church, not having spot, or wrinkle, or any such

> thing; but that it should be holy and without blemish. So ought men to love their wives as their own bodies. He that loved his wife loved himself. For no man ever yet hated his own flesh; but nourished and cherished it, even as the Lord the church: For we are members of his body, of his flesh, and of his bones. For this cause shall a man leave his father and mother, and shall be joined unto his wife, and they two shall be one flesh.

The moderator responded by agreeing with me, then a man spoke and asked to speak with the lady who called herself Simply the Best; that was me. He identified himself as "The Best of Times," and he continued by saying, "Simply the Best?"

I answered, "Yes, the Best of Times."

He continued by saying, "Are you praying for a husband?"

I said "Yes."

He said, "Did God tell you my name?"

I said, "No."

He said, "Do you want me to tell you what God told me?"

I answered, "No! Not on this conference call."

The moderator answered and said, "Tell it, tell it, tell it."

The man continued by saying, "Simply the Best, the Lord said you are an independent woman who loves to maintain your individuality. He also said that you only have to change your name slightly to 'Simply the Best of Times.'"

He continued by saying, "Simply the Best, in life you never get what you deserve—you get what you fight for. I am a fighter, and when I love, I love deeply."

Well, after that proposal, the moderator responded and said, "All we need to do now is to perform the ceremony."

I was stunned and speechless and said nothing. This man proposed to me without knowing who I was or what I looked like. I was flattered. This guy was determined to find out who I was and where I lived. Three days later, we were on the conference call again talking on a different subject, and the Best of Times wanted to speak to Simply the Best again; he wanted to find out if I was local, meaning in the same state where he was, and I was.

He then asked for us to exchange phone numbers, which we did. That was Monday, October 20, 2014. That same night, the Best of Times called me and told me his real name was Jerry Peters. We shared photos, and we liked what we saw, so we moved forward to meet. Jerry and I met for dinner, Thursday, October 23, 2014, at 5:00 p.m. at Grand Lux restaurant. We both liked each other from the moment we met; our dinner date lasted for about five hours. We talked about everything, but most of all we kissed for about two hours constantly standing outside the restaurant.

That night was beautiful, not because of us, but we believed God had smiled on us and said it was our time to meet. We believed we were soul mates from the moment we met. Jerry has the same birthday as my ex-husband, the father of my eight children; however, we know we are soul mates. Jerry visited me every night for one year straight, not missing one night. On our one-year anniversary, we got married: October 18, 2015.

My journey through life has not been a flowery bed of ease. However, I do believe that the struggles in my life has helped to propel me to where I am today. I am excited about the new venture I am on. I know God is not finished with me yet. My goal is to open a home for battered women. I would love to share my story and help to bring hope to the brokenhearted and restoration to the abused. God is faithful. He did it for me, and I know without any doubt, He can do it for *you*!